The Girls in Their Iron Shoes

poems by

Eileen Moeller

Finishing Line Press
Georgetown, Kentucky

The Girls in Their Iron Shoes

For Charlie, Katie, and Emmet, once upon a time, and always

Copyright © 2017 by Eileen Moeller
ISBN 978-1-63534-142-3 First Edition
All rights reserved under International and Pan-American Copyright Conventions.
No part of this book may be reproduced in any manner whatsoever without written permission from the publisher, except in the case of brief quotations embodied in critical articles and reviews.

ACKNOWLEDGMENTS

Publisher: Leah Maines

Editor: Christen Kincaid

Cover Art: "Once Upon A Time", © Su Blackwell, Su Blackwell Studio Ltd., London U.K., http://www.sublackwell.co.uk

Author Photo: Emmet Moeller

Cover Design: Elizabeth Maines

Printed in the USA on acid-free paper.
Order online: www.finishinglinepress.com
also available on amazon.com

Author inquiries and mail orders:
Finishing Line Press
P. O. Box 1626
Georgetown, Kentucky 40324
U. S. A.

Table of Contents

Water Song 1
No 2
Belly Flop 3
Chubby Girl 4
Period 5
Water Nymph 6
Newlyweds 7
Chasm 8
Serenade 9
Wren 10
Parents 11
Mum's the Word 12
Driving Through the Countryside 13
Trio 14
Ash 15
Battered 16
Monster 17
Witness 18
Legend 19
Archaeology 20
Homeless 21
Ephemeral 23
Widow 24
Light 25
Fossils 26
Flare 27
So 28

*Little hut, little hut, turn your back to the trees
and your face to me, please.*

from "Fenist, The Bright Falcon", a Baba Yaga story

Water Song

The river has long green hair
wavering over
its glassy
insistent heart.

The river must have lured
Ophelia this way
as she drifted toward
that smother of a future.

Come wade deep
it sang.

Weave your lonely tresses
in with mine.

No

Toads small as beetles everywhere,
blending in with the dry grass, hopping
away from the little one who wants to catch them.

She runs over to her father for the net,
but he shakes his head, and yanks it away so hard,
she cries big tears, and jumps up and down
on hot coals of thwarted desire.

Spent, she turns away from him,
then bends and cups one in her hands.

Belly Flop

She tilts at the pool's edge,
back wide and round as a hedgehog's,
pointing stubby fingers toward the water
and falling in,
belly first,
belly first,
every time
belly first,
slapping the
water so hard,
the hard water
slapping her
back.

Chubby Girl

Sits
fat as a
caterpillar
in her tiny
room, prying
a huge scab on
her knee up, on
both sides, until
it looks like wings.
She sees a butterfly
where others see
a wound.

Period

A membrane bursts to release an egg,
and the girl surrounding it dreams
of ovaries full of teeth and hair.
She sees a salt Madonna
crying in a corner,
and tears turn to
drops of blood.

Water Nymph

Goes for a swim,
her hair floating
behind her,
a golden wake
that lifts her father
onto his feet,
gets him in for another dip,
while her mother glares
in the shadow cast
by her big straw hat.

Newlyweds

Posies along the hem of her dress,
her bouquet, a little nosegay,
asleep in her lap. Her clasped
hands beneath it,
round as an egg in the nest.

See how hope nestles in at her feet,
her own little gaggle of chicks?

See how promises limn
the bridegroom's body
as he blocks the sun?

Their hands will be
the necks of two white
birds, as they lie awake,
expectant and broody
about the future
that looms like
a loose-hinged
barn door
about to fall.

Chasm

It's like slipping into a warm bath, he says,
when she asks him what it's like when he's inside her.

And what's it like for you? He wants to know.

But she doesn't feel like telling him
about the Milky Way, its helixes of appetite,
stars dying and awakening, its tickles made of light.

Serenade

One time she leaned into a henhouse
and they sang to her, nest-crooned
a harmony of low clucks and high trills.

In it she heard captivity and defiance.

Nothing like the preening screech of the rooster.

More a whoosh of gravel down a hillside,
soft and steady, turning like a luminous
globe in her hands, as she hums
the bones of the only tune she remembers.

Wren

The kids go to camp all week
and a wren sings to her
from the lilac bush.

She hops from branch to
bed to couch to chair,
looking for who
she used to be.

The little house
sways on the branch,
and she's wringing her hands
saying, now what? Now what?

Unable to stand the quiet
any longer, she begins to
hatch a melody, her quick hands
weaving a nest made of feathers and hair.

Parents

Her father called her
mother's breasts his bunnies,
and she wondered if that was why
he kept cuddling their marriage
so close, even after it was dead.

Later, she read that predators
dream more than their prey,
and she came to see him differently—
the gleam in his eye, the shadow
he tried so hard to cast across
her mother's indifference.

Mum's The Word

Why does she stay silent
when she should speak?

Because if she opens her mouth
the flies will get out,
their opalescent insistence
cruising her personal space.

Hundreds of aggregate eyes,
multiplying the garbage
piled between them
here in the silence.

Hundreds of tiny feet,
lighting briefly,
on the face of
her Beloved;
on her own.

Driving Through The Countryside

Every farm has a graveyard,
with a fence around it to keep the cows out.
And the barns that have passed away
are laid out in the fields like broken arks.

Every farm has a house that's neatly plumb,
and inside it a child humming *Away in a Manger*,
as loud as she can, while her parents
shovel some casserole into their mouths,
too tired to tell her to stop.

Trio

Look, a waitress just served
the woman at the next table a hot fudge sundae,
while the man across from her hunches over a glass of water.

And look, they have a son who sits between them.
He's got himself a burger deluxe, and doesn't it look good.
Watch how it takes him away from his mother's
chatter, his father's silence.

And let yourself feel
the pain that blooms in her eyes,
until the boy comes back to reality,
perks up, and lays a funny story down,
like the present it is, on the table in front of her,
while the old man stares out the window.

Ash

Fire signature on a brick wall:
that's what you have left of the mother who fed you,
and kissed, and smoothed your hair,
and slapped you when you were fresh,
now breathless in an ashen sleep.

Post movement, you might say
as they hand you a little urn.

You wander in your grief
through empty fields
for one last gleaning.

Battered

A man breaks a circle of bone with his fist.
He says he doesn't like the way
his woman looks at him.

So she stops looking.
Her eye becomes an absence,
goes stupid, waiting to be torn loose
like a clot from a flooding womb.

And the rest of her
returns to him every time,
their marriage a web of adhesions
tightly winding around her.

Monster

She cleans the wall oven
every time she cooks
because the drippings
look like bruises.
Sees herself
in that dark glass
looking worried
she'll blurt out
what he does to her,
what he makes her do,
her Rebel Without a Cause,
her monster, the only one who
wanted her enough to say the word love.

Witness

Try to pry her loose,
give her respite, offer shelter
when she runs away, listen
full of horror,
pour her a cup of sisterhood,
pray that she'll wake up
to a different life,
have the occasional
breakdown, and beg her
to leave him, knowing this
may cause her to slip
out of reach for
who knows how long?
Like a scab that keeps
coming off, a scream
behind a brick wall
too high to climb.

Legend

The unofficial patron saint of new beginnings
is *La Diffunta Correa:* a sweet young pregnant woman
who went into the Patagonian desert searching
for her vanished soldier husband.

They say that rescuers found her dead,
but full of milk for the newborn,
pink and fat as a piglet,
suckling her icy breasts.

Archaeology

She digs in the sand
with a child's plastic shovel.

She's been doing this for a long time:
searching for the bones of her husband
who was *disappeared* twenty years ago
by a government he couldn't support.

Where is this, you say?
Does it really matter?
Husbands are fading away
everywhere, aren't they?
Don't they fall into mass
graves every morning?
And every evening, don't we
have to patiently dig them out?

Homeless

Her hair is woven
into a solid mass
at the back of her neck,
matted really,
like the clusters of bags
she carries: ballast, so
she doesn't fly away.

She's a wanderer, you say,
her earthly umbilical,
like yours, scissored,
by ignorance, from history.

Keening, unable to light,
she moves across
the landscape,
never a part of it,
and you float
like a lost balloon
above her, hoping
she'll find a tear
in the fabric,
the two of you
might slip through,
back into Paradise.

You read her, you
read her alright—
see the two of you,
like the girl in the fairy tale,
wearing out three
pairs of iron shoes.

You read her, until you
feel tired and helpless.
Then you pick up
your heavy feet
and walk away.

Ephemeral

A woman is stopped next to you
at a traffic light, the setting sun reduced now
to a golden glow on the woman's brown skin.

A little girl is tucked into a car seat behind her
and you see that this woman has to be a mother
because she is holding a tiny ghost in her hand,
the little girl's ghost, and she is kissing it
with a reverence that makes you wish
that you were that little girl
or even her ghost,

and then the light changes
and they leave you stranded
inside your longing,
a spectral wanderer
with nowhere to go.

Widow

She kisses the past:
a perfunctory kiss on fading lips.

For years she kissed her husband like this
when he came home from work,
but now all she has is this collection of moments
that look at her as if they want to do more than kiss.

This shocks her and she blushes
like a fragrant girl
just awakened from her long sleep.

Light

On the top floor of the cancer hospital
a bald woman is playing the piano.

Notes fly like radioactive beams
from her fingers, and the memory of her
gleaming there in the afternoon sun,
will pulse in you, long after,
shrinking all the ugliness, the hard
hard nuggets of darkness
we swallow every day.

Fossils

At eighty-nine she curls
in her nursing home bed
like a seed about to sprout.

She shows no interest
in the television set,
her daughter begs her
to watch to pass the time.

She no longer wants to look
at the photo albums full of children
she doesn't recognize, the knitting
she used to do for them,
shoved in the drawer of the nightstand
along with the gifts, the chalky powders,
the creams separating in their jars,
the candies the aides pilfer
every time they come in.

All fossils now, for someone else to dig up.

Pretty soon you'll be ninety, Ma, they say.
What do you want for your birthday?

Flare

Put your hands over your eyes
because a woman is burning.

You know you are dreaming
but you don't want to see it anyway.

She is burning inside her car and people are screaming.
She is charred black and skeletal
but she rises up nevertheless,
rises up out of the sunroof,
all jubilance and leave taking.

There is nothing to be afraid of, she tells you.
Just like the flare of a match head:
you're here, and then you're gone

So

On the desert's rim
where there is nothing allowed to open,
but dark legs, and grief as stubborn
as wild grass, a woman appears:
her dress, an indigo flower
with slashes of lightning.

But this is not what haunts you.

The nose ring, the earrings,
the lip rings she wears,
all of them catching on the
sharp edges of dreams,
her painful kisses,
not even these
do you carry away
against your will.

Just two things:
the key, her father
plucked from the sand,
worn because
it is beautiful,
and the name her
mother gave her
which is *So*.

Additional Acknowledgements

Though none of these poems have been previously published, I would like to thank the following people for reading and commenting on them: Elizabeth Hays Gatti, who became my sister in our college consciousness raising group, and who has traded poems and ideas with me over forty years of that sisterhood; My aunt, Elaine Matt, who despite her own difficult life, supported me in my journey; Anne Cotgreave, and the Women In Words Writing Group at Riverside Studios, London for much needed encouragement; Martha Rhodes, Leonard Gontarek, and Cindy Day, who read and thoughtfully endorsed the manuscript; and Sean Thomas Dougherty, who so wisely urged me to give each poem enough space to strut its stuff.

Many thanks to Leah Maines, at Finishing Line Press, for bringing this work into the light, to Editor Christen Kincaid, Designer Elizabeth Maines, and to Su Blackwell for her brilliant cut-paper sculpture, "Once Upon A Time" which graces the cover.

Finally, I am grateful for the many women who have traveled alongside me in their iron shoes. or who have shared their moments of transcendence and relief, each one of them a unique embodiment of the Goddess.

Eileen Moeller grew up in Paterson, New Jersey, and has lived in many places with her husband Charles, a psychologist, most recently in Medford, New Jersey. She earned an M.A. in Creative Writing, from Syracuse University in 1991, and taught writing there for fifteen years. She was also a teaching artist for Central New York Community Arts Council, and taught creative writing at local art centers, libraries, at Pratt at MWPI, and at Hamilton College. Her first book, titled *Firefly, Brightly Burning*, was published by Grayson Books in 2015. Her poems have also appeared in anthologies and literary journals, in the United States and in England, most recently in:

Cries of the Spirit: A Celebration of Women's Spiritualty, ed. Marilyn Swell, Beacon Press 1987; *Claiming The Spirit Within: A Sourcebook Of Women's Poetry*, ed. Marilyn Sewell, Beacon Press 1994; *Caprice* 1996; *Writing Women* (England)1997; *Poetry London Newsletter* 1997; *The Nerve: A Writing Women Anthology*, Virago Press, 1997; *Feminist Studies*, Summer 2002 and Spring 2003; *The Paterson Literary Review* 2005; *Paterson: A Poet's City Anthology* 2005; *Blue Fifth Review* (online) 2007; *Comstock Review* 2007; *Philadelphia Stories* 2007; *Women.Period: an anthology* 2008; *Kritya* (online) 2008; *Philadelphia Stories* 2008; *Melusine* (online) 2009; *Fox Chase Review* 2009; *Umbrella* (online) 2009; *The Wild* 2009; *Paterson Literary Review* 2010; *Ars Medica* Spring 2010; *Poems of Awakening*, ed. Betsy Small 2010; A CD, *Snow White Turns Sixty*, by contemporary composer Dale Trumbore 2011; *Ars Medica* Fall 2012; *Sugar Mule* (online) Special Walt Whitman Issue 2012; *Philadelphia Stories* (online); *Philadelphia Stories* (online) Summer 2013; *Schuylkill Valley Journal* Spring 2013; *Grit, Gravity & Grace: New Poems about Medicine and Healthcare* ed. Rhonda L. Soricelli M.D. and Jack Coulehan, M.D., M.P.H., *Mutter Museum of Medical Oddities*, 2015; *50 Over Fifty: A Celebration of Established and Emerging Women Writers* ed. Carla Spataro, PS Books, 2016.

Her blog, *And So I Sing: Poems And Iconography* can be accessed at http://eileenmoeller.blogspot.com

www.ingramcontent.com/pod-product-compliance
Lightning Source LLC
LaVergne TN
LVHW041509070426
835507LV00012B/1433